What's Inside

Trains

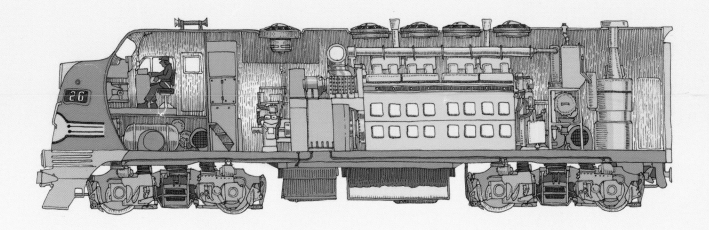

W

FRANKLIN WATTS
LONDON • SYDNEY

Franklin Watts
First published in Great Britain in 2016 by The Watts Publishing Group

Copyright © 2015 David West Children's Books

Designed and illustrated by David West

Dewey number 625.2-dc23
HB ISBN 9 781 4451 4624 9

Printed in Malaysia

Franklin Watts
An imprint of
Hachette Children's Group
Part of The Watts Publishing Group
Carmelite House
50 Victoria Embankment
London EC4Y 0DZ

An Hachette UK Company
www.hachette.co.uk

www.franklinwatts.co.uk

WHAT'S INSIDE TRAINS
was produced for Franklin Watts by
David West 👫 Children's Books, 6 Princeton Court, 55 Felsham Road, London SW15 1AZ

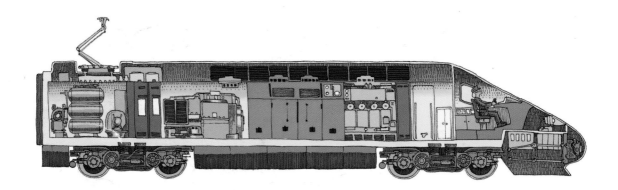

Contents

Steam Trains

The first trains were powered by steam locomotives in the early 1800s. Coal or wood was burnt in a firebox, which heated water in a boiler to make steam. The steam powered **pistons**, which turned the wheels. Water and fuel were stored in the **tender** at the back of the locomotive.

This Peppercorn A1s was able to pull 15 coaches at a speed of 112 kph (70 mph). It had four front wheels, six main wheels and two back wheels and so it was called a 4-6-2 locomotive.

Steam Locomotive

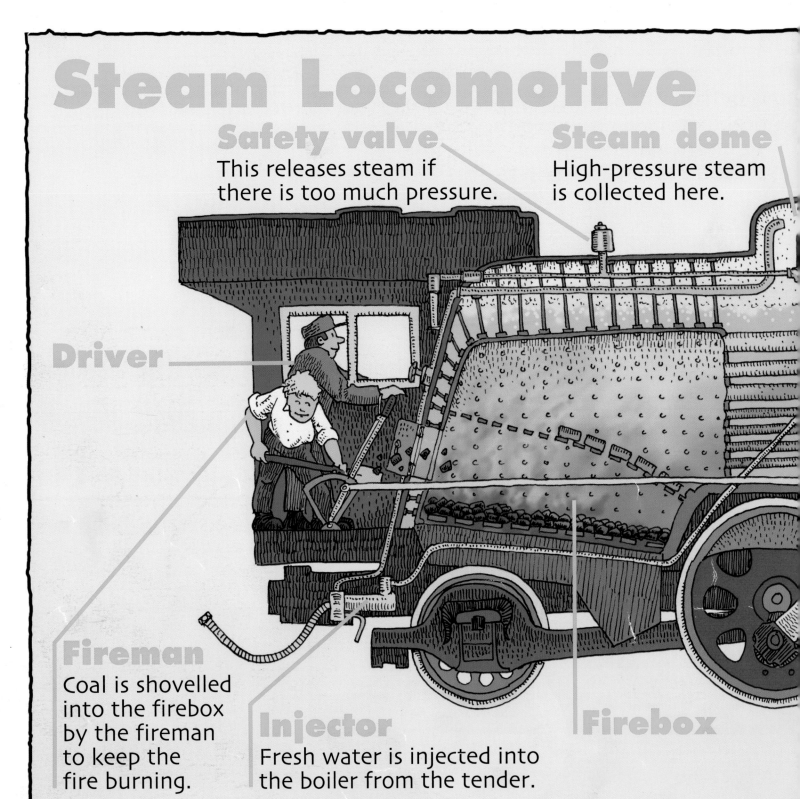

Safety valve
This releases steam if there is too much pressure.

Steam dome
High-pressure steam is collected here.

Driver

Fireman
Coal is shovelled into the firebox by the fireman to keep the fire burning.

Injector
Fresh water is injected into the boiler from the tender.

Firebox

Boiler
Heat from the firebox turns water into high-pressure steam.

Sand dome
Sand can be dropped onto the rails in front of the wheels to help grip.

Chimney

Boiler tubes

Blast pipe
Spent steam from the pistons blasts up through the chimney. Hot, smoky fumes travelling through boiler tubes are pulled up with the steam.

Pistons
High-pressure steam pushes pistons to drive the four drive wheels.

Drive wheels

This Santa Fe F3 diesel electric
locomotive from 1948 has four units.
The two units at either end are cab
units. The driver operates the train from
either of these units.

Diesel powered locomotives eventually replaced steam engines. They use diesel engines to power **generators** that supply electricity to electric **traction motors** on each wheel. Locomotive units can be joined together to make the train more powerful.

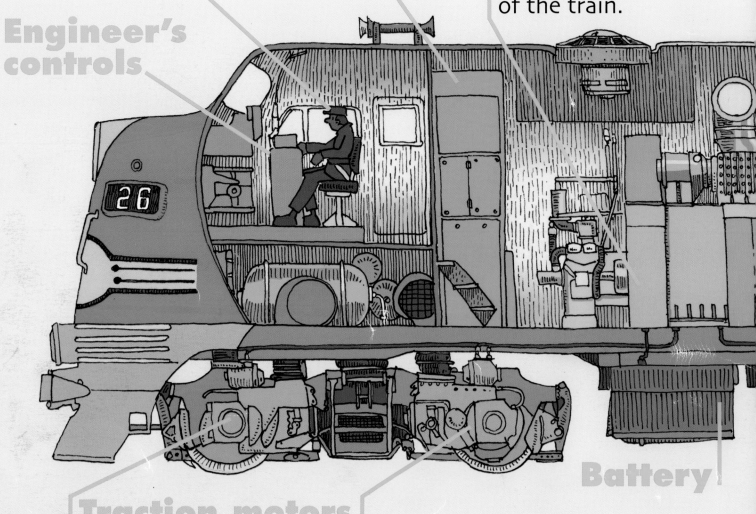

Driver/ Engineer

Electrical cabinet

Generators
Two generators supply electrical power to the traction motors and the rest of the train.

Engineer's controls

Battery

Traction motors

Locomotive

Diesel engine

This supplies power to the electricity generators.

Cooling fans

Water tank

Steam generator

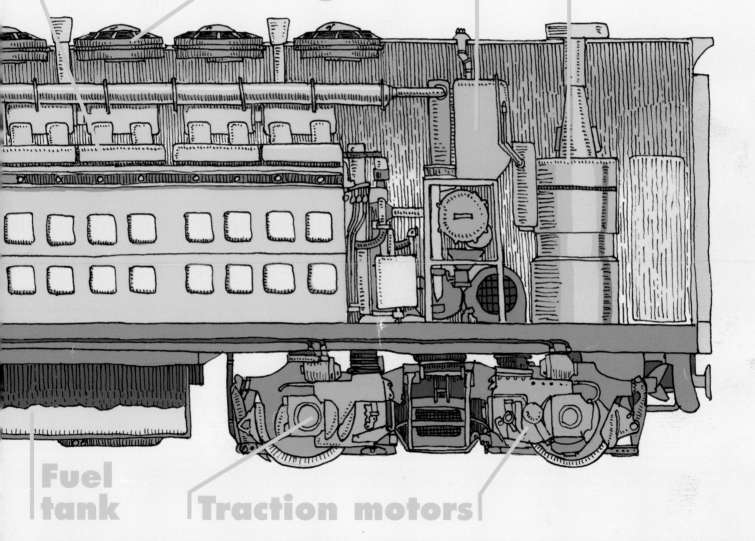

Fuel tank

Traction motors

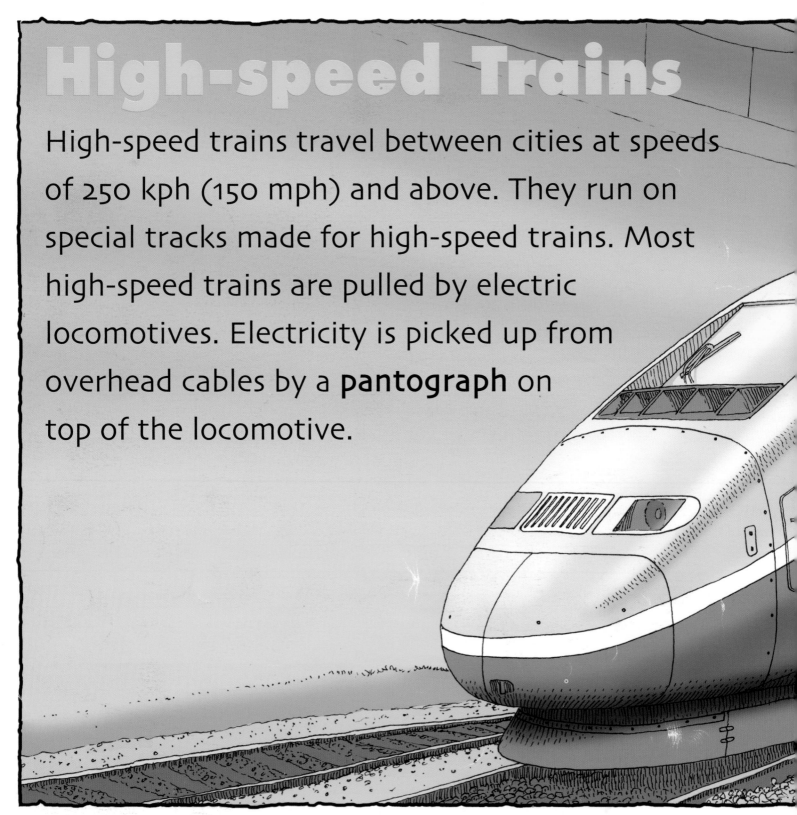

High-speed Trains

High-speed trains travel between cities at speeds of 250 kph (150 mph) and above. They run on special tracks made for high-speed trains. Most high-speed trains are pulled by electric locomotives. Electricity is picked up from overhead cables by a **pantograph** on top of the locomotive.

This French TGV can travel at 575 kph (357 mph), although its average speed during a journey is around 280 kph (174 mph).

High-speed Electric

Pantograph

This picks up electricity from overhead wires.

Control modules

These control the power for the electric traction motors.

Bogie

A bogie has four wheels that are powered by two electric motors.

Main transformer

This converts the electricity for the electric traction motors.

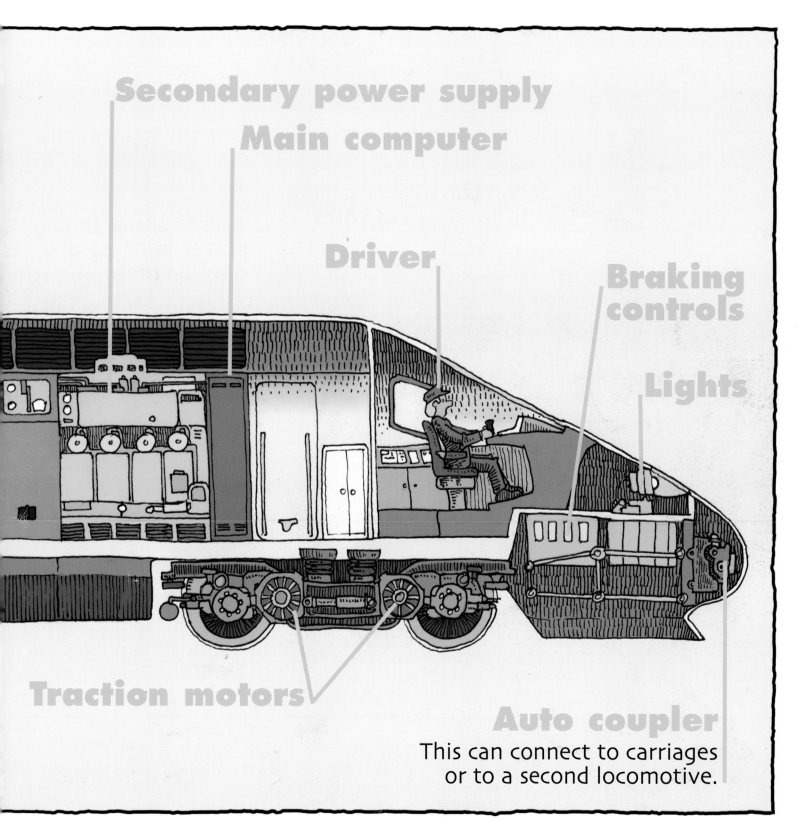

Secondary power supply

Main computer

Driver

Braking controls

Lights

Traction motors

Auto coupler

This can connect to carriages or to a second locomotive.

This SkyTrain in Greater Vancouver, Canada, is fully automated and has no driver. It runs mostly on elevated tracks above the city.

Rapid Transit Trains

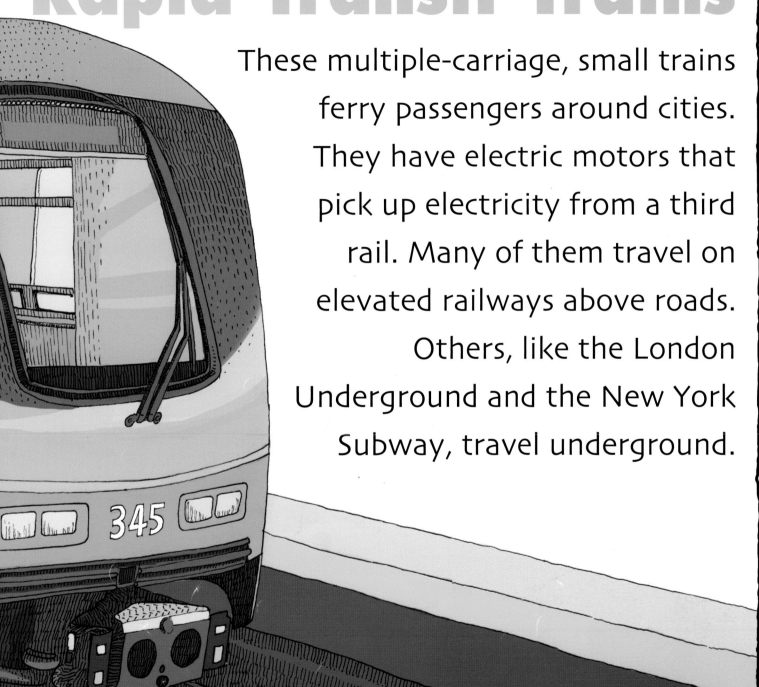

These multiple-carriage, small trains ferry passengers around cities. They have electric motors that pick up electricity from a third rail. Many of them travel on elevated railways above roads. Others, like the London Underground and the New York Subway, travel underground.

Radio antenna
Sends signals to the control centre to show the train's position.

Sliding doors

Gears

Air suspension

Traction motor
The motor turns the wheels through a set of gears.

Urban Metro Train

Sliding doors

Traction motor controls

Power collectors
These collect electricity from the third rail.

Brakes
These use magnets to slow the train down in an emergency.

Many monorail tracks, like this one in Las Vegas, USA, are built high above ground so that they do not interfere with road traffic.

Monorail Trains

Modern monorail trains run on a large, single track. Carriages with rubber wheels straddle a steel, or reinforced concrete beam. They are powered by traction motors, fed by two metal rails that carry electricity.

Monorail

Power unit

Contains a traction motor,
drive wheels and guide wheels.

Passenger compartment

Power collectors

These collect the electricity
from the electric rails that run
along the side of the track.

Transformer

Electricity is sent
to the motors
from here.

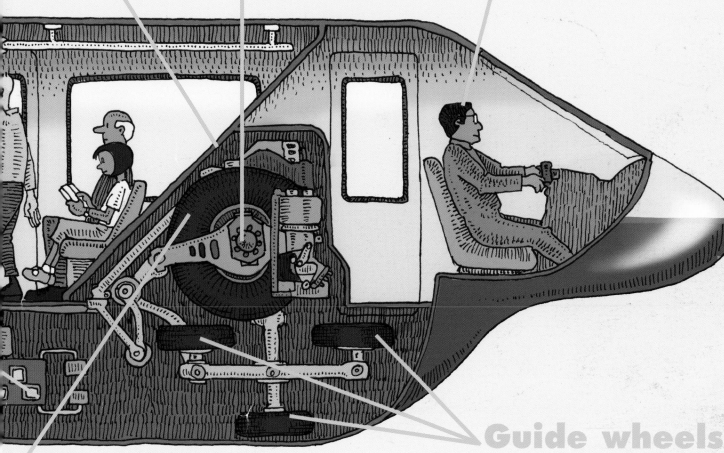

Front power unit

Traction motor
This powers the drive wheels.

Driver

Guide wheels
These run along the side of the track.

Drive wheels
These wheels run along the top of the rail and move the train along the track.

Glossary

generator
A device that converts mechanical power into electricity.

pantograph
A flexible, jointed frame that conveys electricity from overhead wires to a train.

piston
A cylinder, that fits closely in a tube, which is moved backwards and forwards by steam.

tender
A railcar that is coupled to a steam locomotive and carries fuel and water.

traction motor
A powerful electric motor used to move a vehicle, such as an electric train.

Index